I0814948

BY ASHLEY GISH

LA LIGA

BELLWETHER MEDIA · MINNEAPOLIS, MN

Torque brims with excitement perfect for thrill-seekers of all kinds. Discover daring survival skills, explore uncharted worlds, and marvel at mighty engines and extreme sports. In *Torque* books, anything can happen. Are you ready?

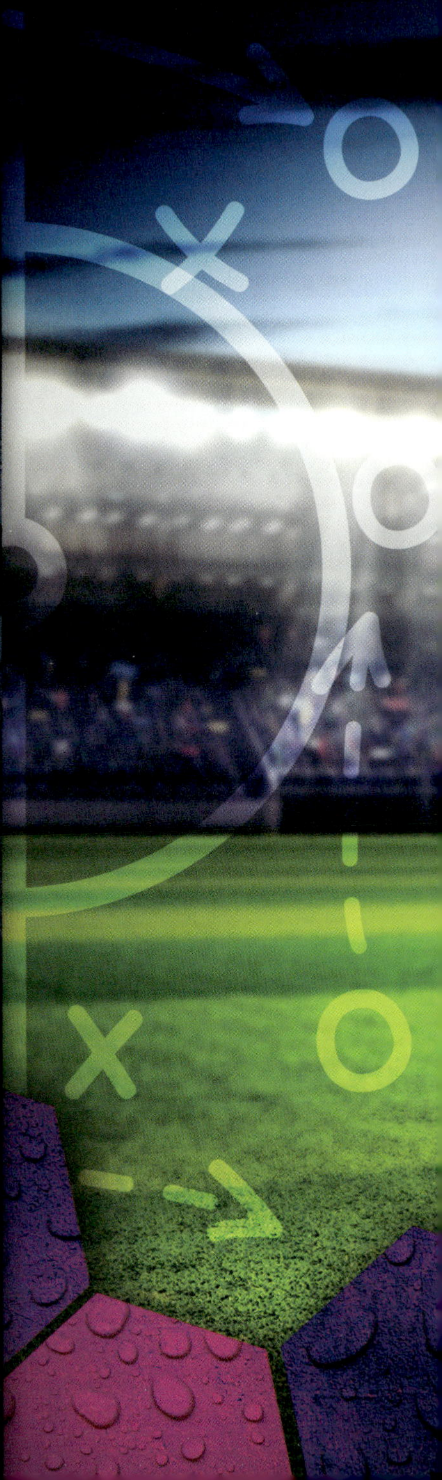

This edition first published in 2025 by Bellwether Media, Inc.

Library of Congress Cataloging-in-Publication Data

LC record for La Liga available at: https://lccn.loc.gov/2024022431

Editor: Kieran Downs   Designer: Gabriel Hilger

Printed in the United States of America, North Mankato, MN.

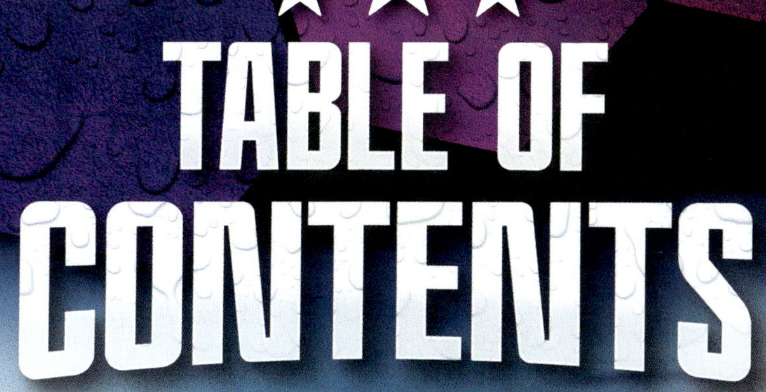

TABLE OF CONTENTS

A GREAT MATCH

It is near the end of the 2023–2024 La Liga season. **Rivals** Real Madrid and Barcelona are playing. Barcelona scores to go up 2–1. But Real Madrid ties the match with a **goal** of their own!

In **extra time**, Real Madrid takes a shot. They score! They have won an important match toward winning La Liga!

REAL MADRID

THE CLASSIC

Any match between Barcelona and Real Madrid is called *El Clásico*, or "The Classic."

WHAT IS LA LIGA?

La Liga is the top soccer league in Spain. The league has 20 teams. Many soccer fans believe La Liga is the best league in the world. Some of the world's greatest players have played in it.

La Liga is known for its **technical** style of play. Its teams are excellent at controlling the ball and making short, quick passes.

HISTORY OF LA LIGA

Before La Liga, the **Copa del Rey** decided who was the best team in Spain. Teams reached the **tournament** from smaller, **regional** leagues. It first took place in Spain in 1903.

In 1927, José María Acha thought Spain should have a national league. The new league would bring the regional leagues together. In 1929, Primera División played its first season.

1903 COPA DEL REY WINNERS

ANOTHER NAME

Primera División is often called La Liga.

FOUNDING TEAMS

La Liga started with 10 teams. Its first **champion** was Barcelona. In 1955, teams from La Liga played against other European teams in the first **Champions League**. Real Madrid won the tournament!

In 1970, La Liga added yellow and red cards. In 1987, the league grew to include 20 teams.

REAL MADRID 1955

TIMELINE

1903

Teams from Spain play in the first Copa del Rey

1929

Primera División, now called La Liga, has its first season

1955

La Liga teams play in the first Champions League

1970 LA LIGA MATCH

1970

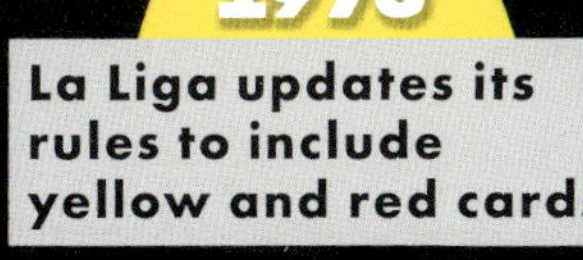

La Liga updates its rules to include yellow and red cards

1987

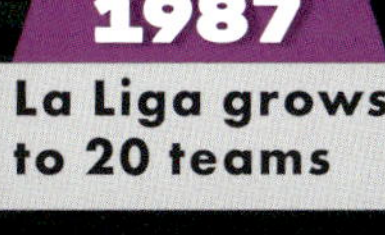

La Liga grows to 20 teams

LA LIGA TODAY

Most La Liga seasons go from August until May the following year. Teams that earned a spot in La Liga the previous season get to play during the current season.

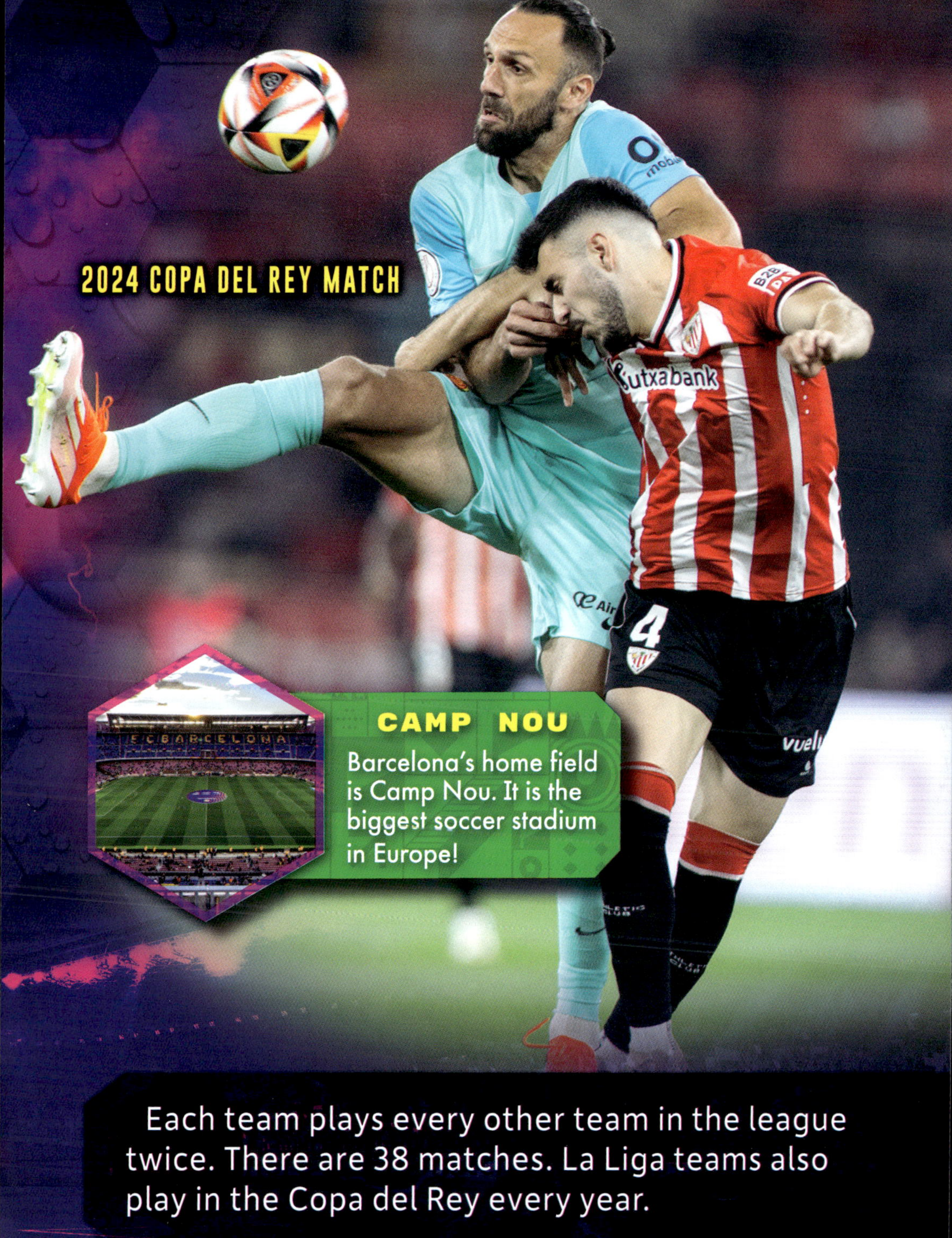

CAMP NOU

Barcelona's home field is Camp Nou. It is the biggest soccer stadium in Europe!

Each team plays every other team in the league twice. There are 38 matches. La Liga teams also play in the Copa del Rey every year.

La Liga championships are based on how well teams play during the season. A win is worth three points. Each team gets one point in a tie. Losing a match is worth zero points.

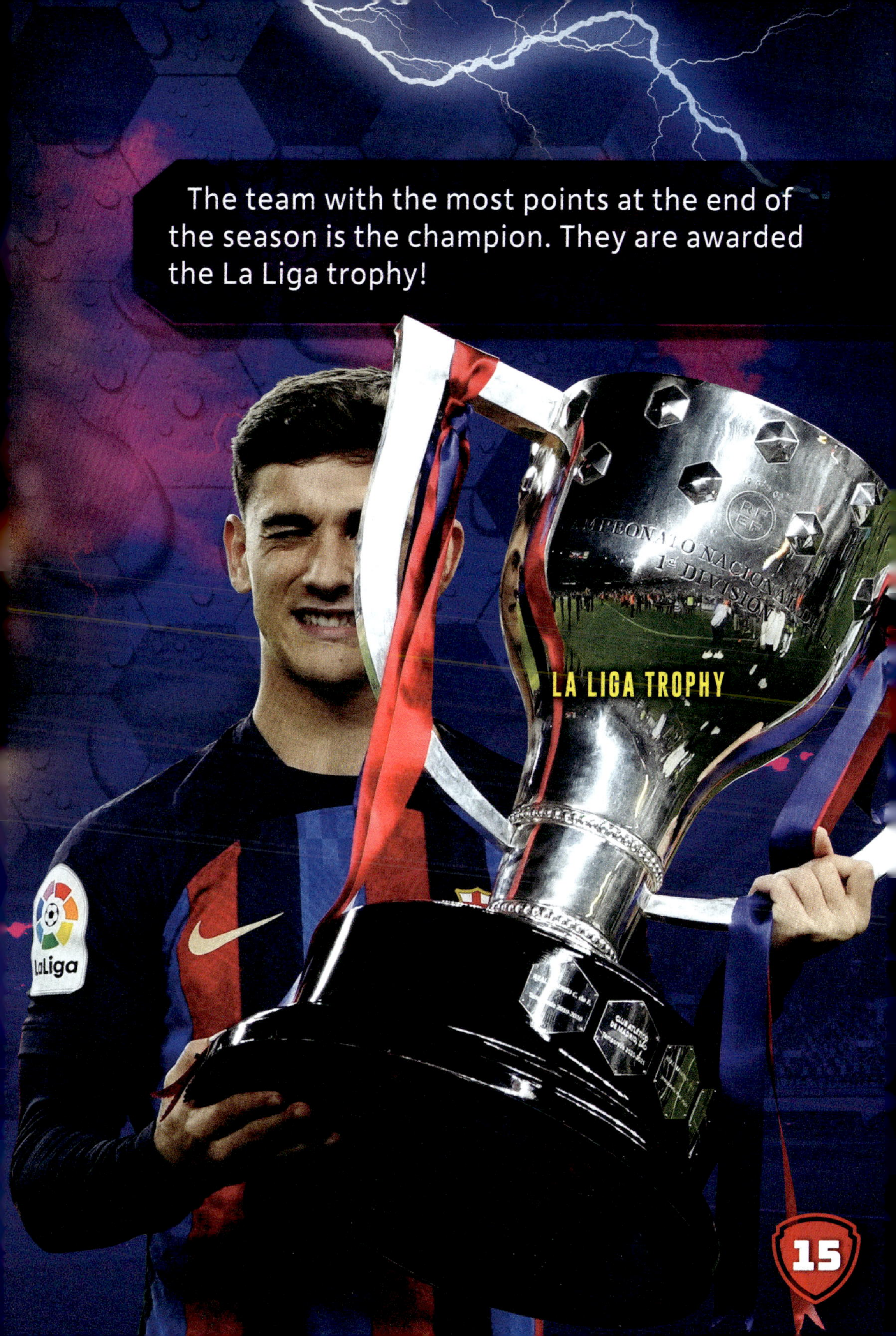
The team with the most points at the end of the season is the champion. They are awarded the La Liga trophy!
LA LIGA TROPHY
LaLiga

Teams are **promoted** and **relegated** to and from La Liga. At the end of each season, the three bottom teams in La Liga are relegated to Segunda División. This league is below La Liga.

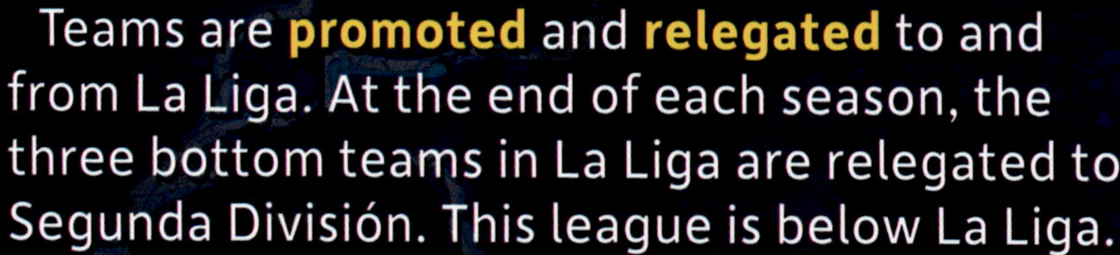

The two top teams in Segunda División are promoted. The teams in third through sixth place play in a **playoff**. The winner is promoted.

2020 PLAYOFF MATCH

RELEGATION AND PROMOTION

1. RELEGATION

The bottom three La Liga teams are relegated.

2. PROMOTION

The top two Segunda División teams are promoted.

3. PLAYOFFS

The teams in third through sixth place play in a playoff. The winner is promoted.

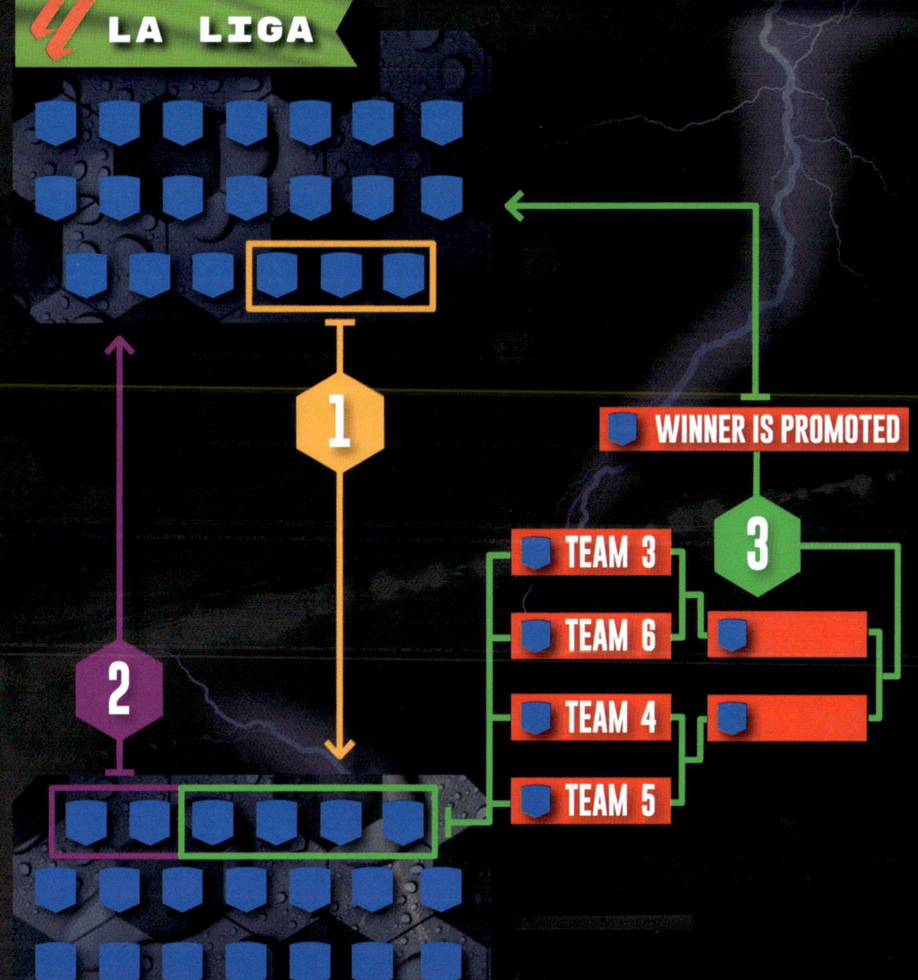

Soccer is a huge part of Spanish **culture**. Fans wear jerseys and face paint. They wave flags. Fans from around the world tune in to matches on TV.

La Liga fans enjoy watching rivals play against each other. The two biggest rivals are Real Madrid and Barcelona. They have played each other over 250 times! La Liga matches are always exciting!

TOP PLAYERS

ALFREDO DI STÉFANO

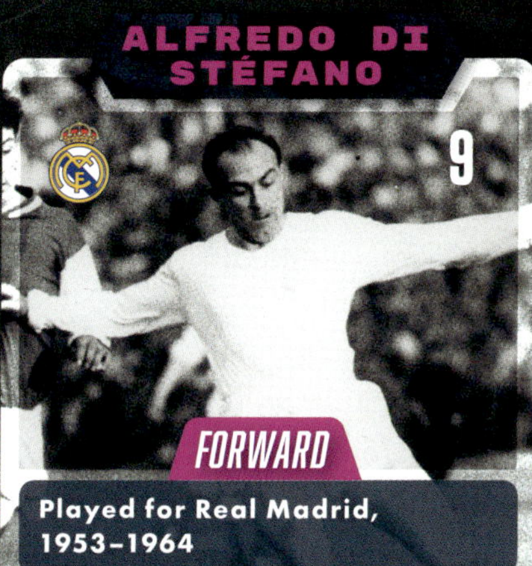

Played for Real Madrid, 1953–1964

XAVI

Played for Barcelona, 1998–2015

Played for Barcelona, 2004–2021

Played for Atlético Madrid, 2007–2011

Played for Real Madrid, 2009–2018

FAST FACTS

NUMBER OF TEAMS	20
YEAR STARTED	1929

LARGEST STADIUM

CAMP NOU

BARCELONA

Capacity: 99,354 people

Location: Barcelona, Spain

CLUB RECORDS
(AS OF 2023)

CLUBS WITH MOST APPEARANCES — 93 seasons
ATHLETIC BILBAO, FC BARCELONA, REAL MADRID

CLUB WITH MOST CHAMPIONSHIPS — 35
REAL MADRID

FIRST CHAMPION
BARCELONA

CLUBS THAT HAVE PARTICIPATED IN THE LEAGUE — 62

INDIVIDUAL RECORDS
(AS OF 2023)

Most career league goals
Lionel Messi:
474 goals

Most goals scored in a single season
Lionel Messi:
50 goals

Fastest goal scored
Joseba Llorente:
7.8 seconds

People with most league appearances
Andoni Zubizarreta and Joaquín:
622 appearances

GLOSSARY

champion—a winner of a contest that decides the best team or person

Champions League—a European soccer tournament where the winners of top European leagues play each other to decide the best team in Europe

Copa del Rey—the championship tournament for professional soccer in Spain

culture—the beliefs, arts, and ways of life in a place or society

extra time—time added to the end of soccer matches to make up for stoppages

goal—a score in soccer; a player scores a goal by sending the ball into the other team's net.

playoff—matches played after the regular season is over; playoff matches determine which teams play in La Liga in the next season.

promoted—moved up to a higher league

regional—related to being from a certain area in a country

relegated—moved down to a lower league

rivals—long-standing opponents that compete for the same thing

technical—related to actions being performed well

tournament—a series of matches in which several teams try to win the championship

TO LEARN MORE

AT THE LIBRARY

Adamson, Thomas K. *Lionel Messi*. Minneapolis, Minn.: Bellwether Media, 2023.

Golkar, Golriz. *Cristiano Ronaldo*. Minneapolis, Minn.: Bellwether Media, 2024.

McDougall, Chrös. *Soccer*. Minneapolis, Minn.: ABDO, 2024.

ON THE WEB

FACTSURFER

Factsurfer.com gives you a safe, fun way to find more information.

1. Go to www.factsurfer.com
2. Enter "La Liga" into the search box and click 🔍.
3. Select your book cover to see a list of related content.

INDEX

The images in this book are reproduced through the courtesy of: PRESSINPHOTO SPORTS AGENCY/ Alamy, cover; Cesar Ortiz Gonzalez/ Alamy, p. 3; Jose Breton/ AP Images, pp. 4, 4-5; Manu Fernandez/ AP Images, p. 5 (The Classic); AFP7 vía Europa Press/ AP Images, pp. 6, 13; David Aliaga/ NurPhoto/ AP Images, p. 7; Unknown author/ Wiki Commons, p. 8 (1903 Copa del Rey winners); NurPhoto/ SRL/ Alamy, pp. 8 (Another Name), 16; La Liga/ Wiki Commons, p. 9; Album/ Alamy, pp. 10 (Real Madrid 1955, 1903, 1929), 11 (1970 La Liga Match); Real Madrid/ Contributor/ Getty Images, p. 10 (1955); Michael Dechev, p. 11 (1970); PA Images/ Alamy, p. 11 (1987); Xinhua/ Alamy, p. 12; ephotocorp/ Alamy, p. 13 (Camp Nou); Jose Breton/ Nur Photo/ AP images, pp. 14, 15; OnTheRoad/ Alamy, p. 18; Sueddeutsche Zeitung Photo/ Alamy, p. 19 (Alfredo Di Stéfano); speedpix/ Alamy, p. 19 (Xavi); PA Images/ Alamy, p. 19 (Lionel Messi, Diego Forlán); dpa picture alliance/ Alamy, p. 19 (Cristiano Ronaldo); ZUMA Press Inc/ Alamy, p. 20; Emre Zengin/ Alamy, p. 21 (Camp Nou); Cesar Ortiz Gonzalez/ Alamy, p. 23.